MIRGONIAN

CODEX

By Mirgonael

First Printing: November 2014

Published and Distributed by Lulu

ISBN: 978-1-312-69449-1

BOOK I

TRAINING

Feeling and Seeing Energy:

Hold your hand up, fingers spread, in front of a dark background. Now, look directly at the center of one of your fingers. You will see a vague, hazy outline extending from the edge of your finger out about a quarter of an inch. Each person sees this differently at first, but they usually appear as hazy blue or white. Sometimes they appear almost clear, but will always be visible. It should only take a few seconds to be able to see this. This is an aura; the natural magickal energy that you will soon learn to control. Now, you will learn how to feel the power.

Hold your hands straight, fingers together, perpendicular to one another (A 90 degree angle). Without letting your fingers touch, pass the fingertips of one hand across the palm of the other. Remember not to actually touch. As the fingertips of one hand move past the palm of the other, you will feel a tingling directly in front of where your fingers are passing. What you are feeling is the energy emanating from your fingertips.

Now, with a partner, hold your hands up, palms forward. Have them hold their hands up as well with their palms about half an inch from yours. Do not actually touch. You will feel a sensation akin to two magnets pushing against one another. What you are feeling is your energy pushing off of your partner's energy. With your hands still palm to palm, look at your aura. You can see your energy has expanded as it reacts to your partner's. Continue to practice seeing and feeling your energy as well as the energy of those around you.

NOTE: How one person sees an aura is not, necessarily, how another will see the same aura. For example, if two people were to look at someone whose aura bears the mark of evil magick, each person would see a color to indicate this. If, to one person, black indicates evil, they would see a black mark across the aura. However, if to the other viewer red is indicative of evil, they would see a red mark. Though they both see something different, they are still viewing the same blemish. Therefore, when viewing auras, do not trust any book or source that tells you what different colors mean when seen. Rather, ask yourself what those colors mean to you.

Channeling Energy:

Sit comfortably in a dimly lit room. Candlelight is ideal for this. Cup your hands together in your lap, and position them so that your palms are in shadow. Now, relax. Remember how the energy felt to your palms in the previous exercises. Now, let yourself feel this same energy with your entire body. Feel the waves of natural power washing over you and around you. Breathe deeply. As you breathe in, feel the energy flowing into you. As you breathe out, let the energy gather between your shoulder blades. This point is a chakara, one of the body's natural power centers. Breathe in, drawing in the energy. Breathe out, and focus the energy between your shoulders.

Continue building up this power until you feel a tingling sensation run through your spine. Now, breathe in, and as you breathe out let the energy between your shoulders flow down your arms and into your hands. Focus this energy into your cupped palms and let it gather there as a ball of energy held between your hands. Continue pulling energy in and focusing it down your arms and into your hands. When you feel a tingling pulse in your palms, open your eyes and look at your hands. The ball of energy in your hands will appear the same as an aura, only much more defined and concentrated. The hazy mist of the energy will be quite visible as your palms rest in shadow.

Now, press your palms flat against one another. Keeping your palms parallel, draw them apart up to six inches. Let the energy flow back and forth between your palms. These waves of rippling energy will also be readily visible. When you are done, be sure to ground yourself. That is to say, place your hands on the ground or floor and let all of the built up energy flow out of you. When you feel your energy level return to normal, take a few deep breaths. This grounding procedure completes this exercise.

Finding One's Strengths:

Now that you know how to tap into sources of magickal energy, it is important to discover your strengths. To do this, you will need a lit candle, a bowl of water, a rock, a plant, a piece of bone, and access to a natural breeze or wind. When using magick, if you are right handed, your left hand is your receiving hand, while your right hand is your power hand. If you are left handed, then these would be reversed for you. If, however, you are ambidextrous, then your power hand is the one wherein you have been able to gather the most energy.

Once you have gathered the required items, sit and calm yourself. Cup your receiving hand around the flame of the lit candle without actually touching the fire. Now, draw in the energy from the flame, and let it flow up your arm, down your other arm, and into your power hand. Once the energy is built up in your power hand, look at that hand's aura. Now, break contact with the flame and ground the energy.

Repeat this process with each of the other elements. For water, place your receiving hand gently in the bowl. For nature, grasp the plant. For earth, lay your hand upon the rock. For air, hold your hand to the breeze. For necromancy, grasp the bone.

Once you have done the exercise will all of these items, compare the results. The source that you gained the greatest amount of power from is your natural element. This is the source you should draw from for most of your magickal practices. Down the road, you can always come back and work to develop your skills with the other elements, but save that hurdle for another time.

NOTE: Once you have determined with what source your strength lies, it would be wise to research that element. This will show you what that element is most commonly used for, and, thereby, suggest to you where to focus your studies. As you delve into the other elements, you can always work with their areas of focus as well.

ADDITIONAL NOTE: This exercise calls for a lit candle. If you do not know how to safely light and use a candle, then you shouldn't be reading this book to begin with.

Shielding:

As you continue to grow in power, you will begin to attract the attention of other mages, as well as extra-planar entities. Some of these will seek you out with less than friendly intentions. Therefore, it is wise to know how to defend yourself. Again, draw in energy, this time from whichever source is your greatest strength. Instead of letting it flow into your hands, however, let it flow out of you in every direction. Will it to form a sphere around you, with you at its center. This will prevent spells and entities from being able to reach you.

The more energy you put into the sphere, the more protected you will be. While this shield will protect you from attacks from any direction, it is weakened by its dispersal. In other words, the magic is spread thinner to cover a larger area, and therein lays its weakness.

Another basic defense is less encompassing, but more concentrated. To create this shield, hold your receiving hand in front of you with your palm forward. Let the energy you gather flow down your arm and through your palm. Will the energy to form a disc centered on your palm, and with a radius of about one foot. This shield is much stronger than the previous one due to the fact that all of the energy is concentrated in one small area. However, it must be held directly in the path of the incoming attack. Practice creating these shields, and let your partner direct his or her energy against them. Experiment with the sensation of another's energy striking your shield, and practice creating the shields quickly. Remember, the faster you can put up a shield, the safer you will be.

Remote Viewing:

For this you will need a sphere made of crystal, glass, or stone; the size is unimportant. Even a sphere the size of a marble will suffice. Sit comfortably with the sphere before you. Close your eyes. Build up some energy; let the energy flow up your spine and into the front of your head. The center of your forehead is known as the Third Eye, and it is here that you must gather the energy. When you feel your Third Eye begins to pulse and tingle, reach out with your mind to the sphere. Some mages visualize this as a tentacle of energy reaching from their forehead and touching the object. Once you establish a strong link, shift your point of perspective forward along the link. Feel yourself drift along the link and into the sphere. Now, instead of looking out from your eyes, try to look up from the sphere. See from the sphere's point of view. If the sphere is on the floor, see the surrounding area from that point on the floor. Once this has been done, withdraw back into your own mind, and break contact. You can also try this with other people. That, however, we will leave to the next exercise.

Mind Linking:

This lesson applies practices learned in the last exercise. For this you will need a partner who can concentrate on an image and ignore distractions. The partner must also be willing, and someone that you trust implicitly. If they are unwilling, the exercise is a great deal more difficult. Additionally, if you do not trust them fully, do not try this with them, for they could gain access to your mind while you are trying to gain access to theirs.

Sit comfortably with your partner sitting about five to six feet away from you. You must also be facing one another. Have your partner concentrate on a setting, such as mountains, woods, a beach, etc. Do not let them tell you what it is. You cannot know in advance or the exercise is ruined. Now, link minds with

them as in the previous exercise.
However, instead of seeing through their
eyes, focus on their thoughts. Let the
images of what they are thinking appear
before you. Once you can see the
setting, break contact and open your
eyes.

Tell them what you saw and confirm
that you got the right image. If you did
not, try again. Once you can get the
image perfectly, you will be able to see
what you had done wrong with the
previous attempts, and what it took to
correct them. Practice this exercise
repeatedly until the link can be
established quickly and with great
accuracy. At this point, you will be able
to link minds with unknowing partners and
read their thoughts.

NOTE: As mentioned about trust,
be very careful with linking minds with

others. You never know when the random person who's mind you are attempting to read may turn out to be a fellow practitioner. If that is in fact the case, you had better hope that they are not offended by your intrusion, or else you may discover, rather unpleasantly, that they have a little more experience than yourself.

Weather Control:

Now that you have experimented with drawing in energy and directing it outward, it is time to move on to a more generalized form of external magick. When manipulating the weather, keep in mind that nature will always create a balance. For example, if you pull a rain storm to you, you may be leaving another area to drought. If you push away all wind from one area, you may be delivering tornadoes to another. These are extreme examples, but they are not unheard of.

To begin, tap into your preferred source of power, and draw in as much energy as you feel you will need. Now, reach out, up, and away from yourself. Send the gathered energy into the sky to find the weather type you seek. Then, draw the energy back to yourself and bring the weather with it.

When summoning wind, the effect is instantaneous. Rain storms have been found to take about one hour if one already exists to be drawn to you. If, however, one needs to be created, then they have been found to take almost exactly four hours to create and call forth. Hurricanes, unfortunately, always take three days. It is not known why, exactly, but none that I have ever met have been able to bypass this timeframe.

These times, however, are not how long you must sit there casting the spell. The casting of the spell takes moments only. Once cast, let the energy go and ground yourself. Then, give the magick time to run its course.

NOTE: Only through practice, experimentation, trial, and error will we ever be able to break the laws which bind us and move on to greater magicks.

Therefore, if you believe you can find a way around these times, by all means, may your Art open unto you wondrous new realities.

BOOK II

SPELLS

Casting Spells with Sigils:

1) Draw in energy to power the spell.

2) Visualize the final effect of the spell.

3) Visualize the spell's sigil, and impose the image of the sigil over the image of the spells effect so that they combine in your mind.

4) Chant the spell's incantation while channeling the gathered energy into the visualization.

5) As you complete the incantation, release the energy from the visualization, and out into the world.

Casting Spells without Sigils:

1) Draw in energy to power the spell.

2) Visualize the final effect of the spell.

3) Chant the spell's incantation while channeling the gathered energy into the visualization.

4) As you complete the incantation, release the energy from the visualization, and out into the world.

ACCELERATE

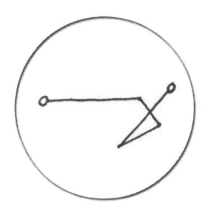

Incantation: Agam Anu Eset!

Pronunciation: Ah–gahm Ah–nu Eh–
set

EFFECT: Casting this spell causes the subject's mind and body to speed up, enabling them to move, think, and react faster than normal for a short time.

ABSORB DWEOMER

Incantation: Teta Ars Astan Asarat Anu!

Pronunciation: Teh-tah Ars Ah-stahn Ah-sah-raht Ah-noo

EFFECT: This spell causes any spells directed at the caster to be converted into raw magickal energy and absorbed by the mage.

ANTI-DISPEL

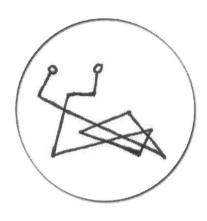

Incantation: Teta Ars Astan Nas Kir Miranus!

Pronunciation: The-tah Ars Ah-stahn Nahs Keer Mee-rah-noos

EFFECT: The spell makes the next spell cast much more difficult to dispel.

BANISH SPIRITS

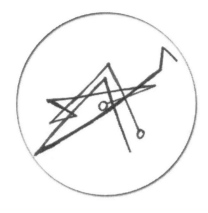

Incantation: Remi Ad Enon!

Pronunciation: Reh-mee Ahd Ee-non

EFFECT: This spell causes any spiritual entities it is directed at to be forced completely from the Material Plane and onto the Astral Plane.

CALL RAIN

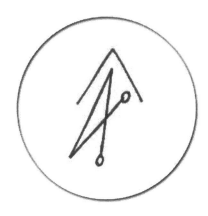

Incantation: Arn Tho Atuste Dasun!

Pronunciation: Arn Thoe Ah–too–steh Dah–soon

EFFECT: This spell summons a rain storm. The speed in which it arrives depends on the focus of the caster.

CALM WIND

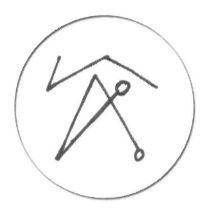

Incantation: Teta Ars Nedi Tho Tarn!

Pronunciation: Teh-tah Ars Neh-dee Thoe Tah-rehn

EFFECT: This spell dispels wind, and causes the surrounding air to calm.

CAUSE NIGHTMARES

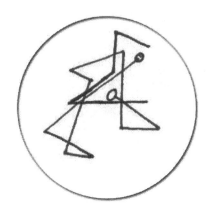

Incantation: Teta Ars Terenta Eranterna Tho Tarn!

Pronunciation: Teh-tah Ars Teh-rehn-tah Er-ahn-ter-nah Thoe Tah-rehn

EFFECT: This spell causes the target to suffer horrible nightmares when next they sleep.

CHARGE

Incantation: Sathetut Ars Tenos!

Pronunciation: Sah-theh-toot Ars Teh-nos

EFFECT: This spell imbues the target object with raw magickal power.

CHILL

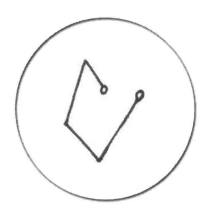

Incantation: Teta Anin Tho Nas Lid Ru Feter!

Pronunciation: Teh-tah Ah-neen Tho Nahs Leed Roo Feh-ter

EFFECT: This spell causes a localized drop in the perceived temperature centered on the caster.

CLAIRAUDIENCE

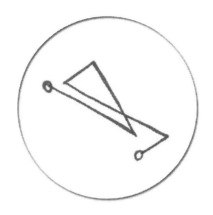

Incantation: Teta Anu Sanast!

Pronunciation: Teh-tah Ah-noo Sah-nahst

EFFECT: This spell causes the caster's hearing to become heightened for the duration of the spell.

COIN SHIELD

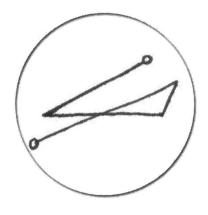

Incantation: Teta Ars Anel Nas
Asondu!

Pronunciation: Teh-tah Ars Ah-nehl
Nahs Ah-son-doo

EFFECT: This spell creates a
temporary magickal shield centered
upon a target coin. The coin can
then be passed on to protect another.

CONFUSION

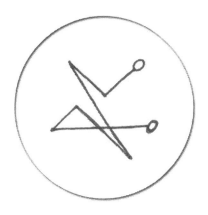

Incantation: Teta Rerasne Tho Serloty Ars Dator!

Pronunciation: Teh-tah Reh-rahs-nee Thoe Sehr-loh-tee Ars Dah-tor

EFFECT: This spell causes the target to become temporarily confused.

DEFENSE

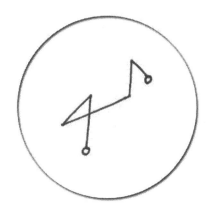

Incantation: Toltorn Od Gah Bolp Ialpor!

Pronunciation: Tohl-torn Ohd Gah Boh-lehp Ee-ahl-pohr

EFFECT: This is a generic defense spell which causes a random defensive effect beneficial to the target of the spell.

DETECT LIFE

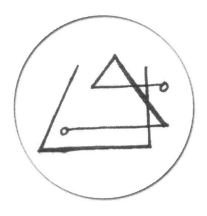

Incantation: Uron Tho Nas Benef!

Pronunciation: Oo-ron Thoe Nahs Beh-neff

EFFECT: This spell enables the caster to sense the presence of any living being within range of the spell effect. This range is determined by the power of the mage.

DISCERN TRUTH

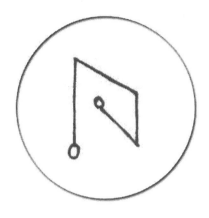

Incantation: Bilar Nas Benef!

Pronunciation: Bee-lar Nahs Beh-nef

EFFECT: The spell enables the caster to sense when the person to whom they are speaking is lying.

DISMISS RAIN

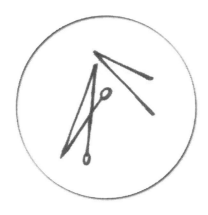

Incantation: Arn Atuste Tho Tarn!

Pronunciation: Arn Ah-toos-teh
Thoe Tah-rehn

EFFECT: This spell causes rain in
the immediate area to relent and halt
altogether.

DISPEL

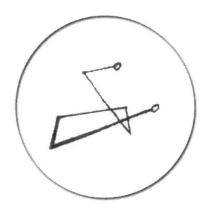

Incantation: Teta Ars Astan Nas Miransh!

Pronunciation: Teh-tah Ars Ah-stahn Nahs Mee-rah-nesh

EFFECT: This spell will dispel any enchantment it is cast upon, so long as the caster of Dispel is stronger than the caster of the enchantment.

DISPEL DEMONIC TAINT

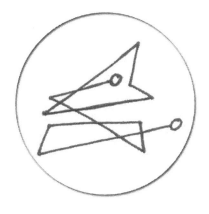

Incantation: Medasrinat Tho Nas Alne!

Pronunciation: Meh-dahs-ree-naht Thoe Nahs Ah-leh-neh

EFFECT: This spell, when cast upon either a person or object, will dispel any demonic taints present.

DWEOMER BLAST

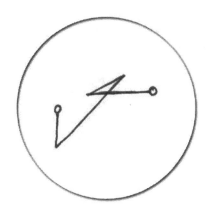

Incantation: Lansh!

Pronunciation: Lah−nehsh

EFFECT: This spell release a blast of raw magickal energy directly at the spell's target.

EMPATHY

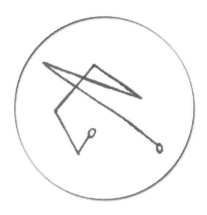

Incantation: Ars Terent Onelrept Tho Nas Benef!

Pronunciation: Ars Teh-rent Oe-nehl-reh-pet Thoe Nahs Beh-nef

EFFECT: This spell enables the caster to sense the surface emotions of those around him for a short time.

ENCHANT BLADE

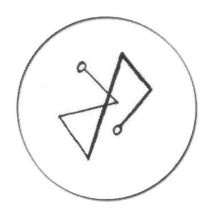

Incantation: Teta Ars Desut Tho Parn Sunoso!

Pronunciation: Teh-tah Ars Deh-soot Thoe Par-neh Soo-noe-soe

EFFECT: This spell temporarily imbues any blade with magickal energy which will help guide it to its target.

END NIGHTMARES

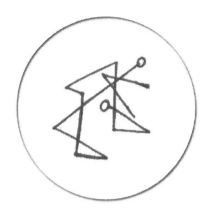

Incantation: Teta Ars Terenta Eranterna Tho Tarn!

Pronunciation: Teh-tah Ars Teh-rehn-tah Eh-rahn-tehr-nah Thoe Tar-neh

EFFECT: This spell brings an end to any nightmares being suffered by the target.

ENHANCEMENT

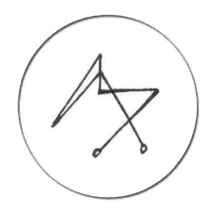

Incantation: Se Gorena Su Nas
Asarat Ars Astan!

Pronunciation: Seh Goe-reh-nah Soo
Nahs Ah-sah-raht Ars Ahs-tahn

EFFECT: This spell causes the next
spell cast to be more effective.

EVERSTRONG

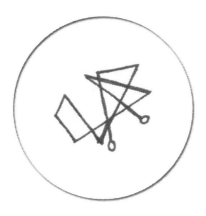

Incantation: Teta Ars Astan Nas Rir Sunertar!

Pronunciation: Teh-tah Ars Ah-stahn Nahs Reer Soo-neh-reh-tahr

EFFECT: This spell causes the next spell cast to become all but permanent.

FERTILITY

Incantation: Tho Af Ero Nas Asitile!

Pronunciation: Thoe Nahs Ee-roe Nahs Ah-see-tee-leh

EFFECT: This spell causes any woman it is cast upon to become more fertile for a short period of time.

FESTER

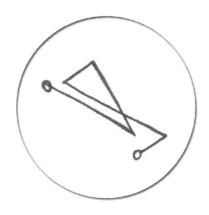

Incantation: Teta Ars Ernus Tenesa!

Pronunciation: Teh-tah Ars Eh-reh-noos Teh-neh-sah

EFFECT: This spell causes any wound it is cast upon to become infected and fester far more quickly than is natural.

GUIDENCE

Incantation: Hirast Ru Dinefe Arde Anu!

Pronunciation: Hee-rah-seht Roo Dee-neh-feh Ah-reh-deh Ah-noo

EFFECT: If lost, this spell enables the caster to sense the direction to his desired destination.

HATE

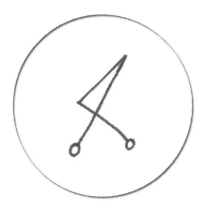

Incantation: Teta Asant Tho Seth Saran Neras!

Pronunciation: Teh-tah Ah-sah-neht Thoe Sehth Sah-rahn Neh-rahs

EFFECT: This spell causes the target to be filled with hatred for the person they are dealing with at that moment.

HEAL

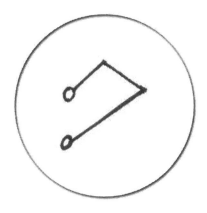

Incantation: Uzug Od Apila Saga!

Pronunciation: Oo-zoog Ode Ah-pee-lah Sah-gah

EFFECT: This spell amplifies the caster's natural healing abilities, thereby enabling them to more effectively heal others.

HELP

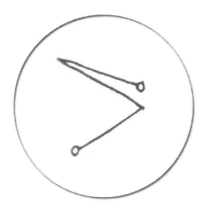

Incantation: Edren Alar Sin Anu!

Pronunciation: Eh-deh-rehn Ah-lahr Seen Ah-noo

EFFECT: This spell calls on the nearest allied entity to help the caster in whatever situation he is in at the moment of casting.

INCREASE EFFECT AREA

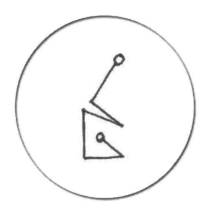

Incantation: Teta Ars Astan Stanuh Doni!

Pronunciation: Teh-tah Ars Ah-stahn Stah-noo Doe-neel

EFFECT: This spell causes the next spell cast to affect a larger area than normal, thus enabling a single-target spell to affect a group of targets.

LOCATE

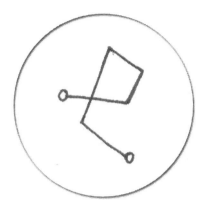

Incantation: Teta Ars Tho Nas Stund!

Pronunciation: Teh-tah Ars Thoe Nahs Stoo-nehd

EFFECT: This spell enables the caster to sense the location of whatever object he is visualizing at the time of casting.

MADNESS

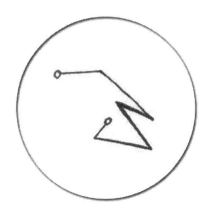

Incantation: Teta Ars Terent Tho Nas Resath!

Pronunciation: Teh-tah Ars Teh-reh-neht Thoe Nahs Reh-sah-teh

EFFECT: This spell causes the target to lose his grip on reality and be driven mad for a brief time.

MANIPULATE

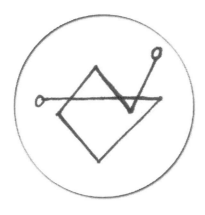

Incantation: Teta Ars Terent Tho Onir Anu!

Pronunciation: Teh-tah Ars Teh-reh-neht Thoe Oe-neer Ah-noo

EFFECT: This spell enables the caster to plant a single thought or action into the mind of the target.

MISPLACE

Incantation: Teta Ars Tho Nas Rab!

Pronunciation: Teh—tah Ars Thoe Nahs Rahb

EFFECT: This spell causes the target to misplace whatever object the caster visualizes at the moment of casting.

NIGHTVISION

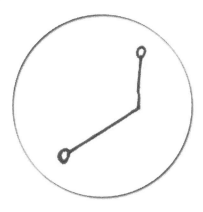

Incantation: Stetlanath!

Pronunciation: Steh-teh-lah-nahth

EFFECT: This spell augments the caster's vision for a short time, enabling him to see more clearly in the dark.

POWERDRAIN

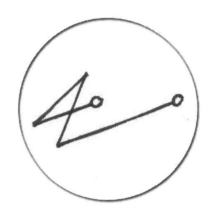

Incantation: Lonshi Torzu Od Pidzar!

Pronunciation: Loe-neh-shee Toe-reh-zoo Oed Pee-deh-zahr

EFFECT: This spell causes all magickal energy to drain out of the target person or object.

PROTECTION FROM DEMONS

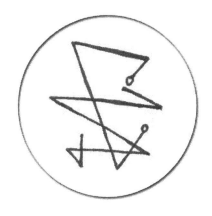

Incantation: Teta Medast Nas Sunerth Des Dirth!

Pronunciation: Teh-tah Meh-dah-seht Nahs Soo-neh-rehth Dehs Dee-rehth

EFFECT: This spell creates a magickal barrier that protects the target from demonic attack.

PROTECTION FROM DRAIN

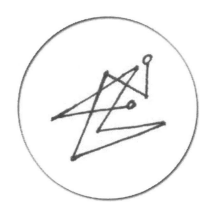

Incantation: Faset Anu Datiril Ratir

Pronunciation: Fah-seht Ah-noo
Dah-tee-reel Rah-teer

EFFECT: This spell creates a
magickal barrier around the target,
temporarily shielding them against all
forms of energy drain.

RAISE SPIRITS

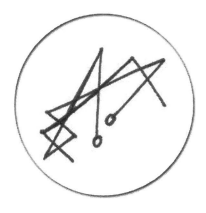

Incantation: Sahan Des Onir

Pronunciation: Sah-hahn Dehs Oe-
neer

EFFECT: This spell calls forth any
spiritual entities within ranges of the
spell, and directs their full attention
to the caster of the spell.

READ THOUGHTS

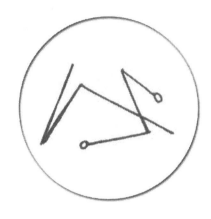

Incantation: Ars Terent Sinal Nas Benef!

Pronunciation: Ars Teh–reh–neht See–nahl Nahs Beh–nehf

EFFECT: This spell enables the caster to sense the surface thoughts of the target of the spell for a short time.

REDIRECT

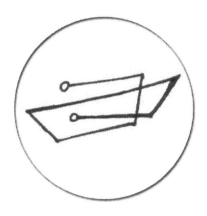

Incantation: Teta Ars Astan Atirte Ars Terent!

Pronunciation: Teh-tah Ars Ah-stahn Ah-teer-teh Ars Teh-reh-neht

EFFECT: This spell causes any spell targeted at the caster to be redirected to a target of the caster's choice.

SENSE DEMONIC TAINT

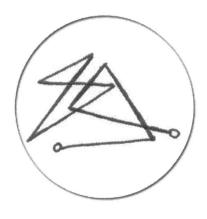

Incantation: Medasrinat Nas Benef!

Pronunciation: Meh-dahs-ree-naht Nahs Beh-nehf

EFFECT: This spell enables the caster to sense the presence of demonic taint for a short time.

SENSE MAGICK

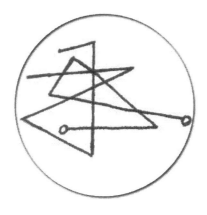

Incantation: Dasrut Tho Nas Benef!

Pronunciation: Dah-seh-root Thoe Nahs Beh-nehf

EFFECT: This spell enables the caster to sense the presence of magickal enchantments for a short time.

SHIELD

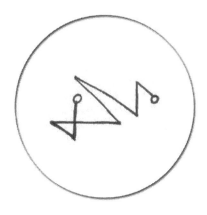

Incantation: Bitom Blans Ol!

Pronunciation: Bee-toem Blah-nehs Oel

EFFECT: This spell creates a temporary magickal shield around the target of the spell.

SPIRIT SIGHT

Incantation: Teta Hirast Tho Nas Anen!

Pronunciation: Teh-tah Hee-rah-seht Thoe Nahs Ah-nehn

EFFECT: This spell grants the caster the ability to see spiritual entities for a short time.

TAP

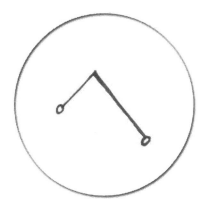

Incantation: Lonshi Ol Geh Deh!

Pronunciation: Loe-neh-shee Oel Geh Deh

EFFECT: This spell drains the power from any targeted object, and funnels the power into the caster.

TOME ENCHANTMENT

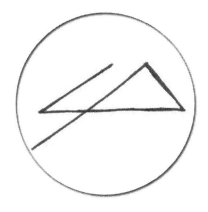

Incantation: Urch Arphe!

Pronunciation: Oo-rehk Ah-reh-feh

EFFECT: This spell creates a permanent shield around any single book, preventing it from being molested by any form of magick.

VAMPIRIC AURA

Incantation: Anu Sura Tho Mires Sten Enar!

Pronunciation: Ah-noo Soo-rah Thoe Mee-rehs Stehn Eh-nahr

EFFECT: This spell surrounds the caster with an aura which will drain power from those around him, absorbing it into himself.

VULNERABILITY

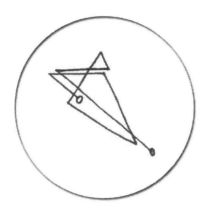

Incantation: Teta Ars Asondu Nas Alne

Pronunciation: Teh-tah Ars Ah-son-doo Nahs Ah-leh-neh

EFFECT: This spell enables the caster to see exactly which point of his enemy is vulnerable to attack at the moment of casting.

WARMTH

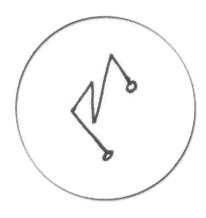

Incantation: Teta Anin Tho Nas Falth Ru Alher!

Pronunciation: Teh-tah Ah-neen Thoe Nahs Fah-lehth Roo Ah-leh-hehr

EFFECT: This spell causes a localized raise in the perceived temperature centered on the caster.

WIND

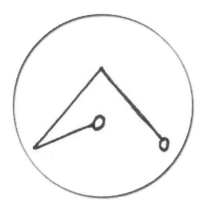

Incantation: Salane Neda Hestal!

Pronunciation: Sah-lah-neh Neh-dah Heh-seh-tahl

EFFECT: This spell conjures a sudden burst of wind which can be directed by the caster.

EMPOWERMENT SPELLS

To renew Powers:

> Verbena hastate
>
> Quattuor elementa
>
> Quattor loci
>
> Hasta verbena
>
> Viam monstra

To increase one's own power:

> Rogorodoron!

To call power from the moon:

> Diana
>
> Luna
>
> Lucina
>
> Lumen
>
> Lumen
>
> Lumen

AUGMENTATION SPELLS

To increase Tarot effectiveness:

> GIBBILANNU

To boost telepathy and divination abilities:

> MASHSHANANNA

To bestow agility and acuity:

> AGNIBAAL

To augment precognition:

> ARATAAGARBAL

To augment combat skill:

> Agnibaal
>
> Lugalabdubur!

To augment scrying ability:

By blessed moon, by faery spell,

By mysteries which here do dwell,

Dreams, desires, arcane might,

Borne on moonbeam's silver light.

Clearest visions, let me see.

Blessed moonlight come to me.

To augment yourself in all things:

Virtue be mine, from faery tree.

Wisdom be mine, from owl born free.

Power be mine, from storm tossed sea.

Beware the fire I cast at thee.

HEALING SPELLS

To heal an injury:

> Light, Beff,
>
> Cletemati, Adonai,
>
> Cleona, Flcrit.

To cure an illness:

> Great fire, my defender and
> protector, son of the celestial
> fire, equal of the sun which
> cleanses the earth of foulness,
> deliver this man/woman from
> the evil sickness that torments
> him / her night and day.

To promote healing and vitality:

> ANNDARABAAL

To heal wounds:

> Happir
>
> Amaosi
>
> Paraop
>
> Poarap
>
> Isoama
>
> Rippah

To heal and protect:

> Sator
>
> Arepo
>
> Tenet
>
> Opera
>
> Rotas!

SHIELDING SPELLS

To shield during a journey:

Argentum vivum,

Clipeus ornatus,

Argentum signatum,

Mercurius argenteus

Tege, Tege, Tege.

To be protected from attack:

Shamash before me

Sin behind me

Nergal at my right

Ninibat at my left

To enchant a shielding stone:

Evil spells you shall deny.

Send it to the earth and sky.

Send it to the flame and sea.

Stone of power, shelter me.

To shield property against theft:

Doer, doer,

Passer by, passer by,

Turn not they face backwards.

Beware the great door.

To protect a home from magickal attack:

BANMASKIM

DEMON-SPECIFIC SPELLS

To banish demons:

> Thou evil thing
>
> Of darkness born,
>
> Or tail and wing
>
> And snout and horn,
>
> Fly from me
>
> From now till morn,
>
> And ever after
>
> Be forlorn.

To be protected when invoking demons:

> ARRA

To conjure a demon:

> (Demon's name) Heloy Tau
>
> Varaf Panthon Homnorcum
>
> Elemiath Serugeath Agla
>
> On Tetragrammaton Casily.

To summon a demon guardian for your home:

Creature of Rage, Creature of Ire,

Born of the flame which rose from the Sea,

Guarding my portals be all thy desire,

Who treads o'er my threshold must answer to thee!

Fear be thine sword, and horror thine sire,

My Will be Thine Will, and now so it be!

To enchant daggers to slay demons:

Eftach mef maliente perjorum

Est mas mal maliente enefnoch

Est. Malmach maliente.

Malmach majorum. Malmach

Mas perjorus.

To enchant opals to shield against demons:

Serviente mest majora.

Serviente mest major.

To cleanse demonic taint:

    Esdach mifmiado endore melmiento est.

    Kasdach mifmiado estiente goromun est.

    Eltach miente bestaman est.

To dominate a succubus:

    Amnot torte vack muhn, fither!

To ward against demons:

    Lictus santu halfnoch diente.

    Lictus santu halfnoch diente.

    Mesta pesora rictus vemt.

To slay a darkling:

    Masshangergal

    Suhrim!

SPIRIT-SPECIFIC SPELLS

To employ dark spirits:

> Lamiae
>
> Larvae
>
> Lemures
>
> Passim, Passim!

To summon a specific spirit:

> From ash and bone
>
> And coil free,
>
> Deathbound spirit
>
> Come to me.
>
> Bring thee now
>
> From Odin's Hall,
>
> As I summon,
>
> Heed my call!

To call a familiar spirit into a dog:

> Cusis, Cusis!

To greet spirits peacefully:

Palifasta Firmis Demecha Haim.

To bind a spirit:

Deus Pata binde Jesus

Behalte Deus Spiritum

Binde durch Kraft Christi

Knuepfe schliesse

(spirit's name) Amen.

To force a spirit to answer questions truthfully:

O Sa miha Aseffonila Ja La Mifflahi

Mehahinesi Milonahireil.

To dismiss a spirit:

O Spirit (spirit's name)

Portam Benedictam Sic

Tecum quasia horas siece

Mila Amen.

To banish a spirit:

> Benedictus est qui Omnia
>
> Regnat per Omnia secula
>
> Seculorum in nominaedomini
>
> Amen.

To summon an evil spirit:

> O Lama Basulai Monai
>
> Mempis Lorrate Pacem.

To imprison an entity:

> Barerimu
>
> Irkingu!

OFFENSIVE SPELLS

To cause impotence:

> Far si far, fa far fay u,
> far four na fourty Kay
> U Mack straik it, a pain
> four hun creig wel Mack
> Smeoran bun bagie.

To dominate another:

> Nux nox
> Pax pox
> Hex hax
> Wix wax
> Hithero hothero
> Withero wothero
> Well.

To dominate a maiden:

Bestarberto corrumpit viscera ejus mulieris.

To control an enemy:

> Malefa
>
> Alefac
>
> Lefact
>
> Efacto
>
> Factor

To decrease an enemy's power:

> Norodarogor!

To cause conflict between others:

> Kanna Aqai Nata
>
> Niaqa A!

To slay an enemy:

> Cased Azote
>
> Boros Etosa
>
> Debac!

To ruin a target's possessions:

> Biniam Inuusi Biniam!

To curse a marriage:

> As this marriage is begun
>
> I curse it till it comes undone.
>
> Knots of anger, knots of hate,
>
> Make unhappiness their fate.

To kill an enemy:

> Xapeth, Xith, Xandra,
>
> Zaped, Zapoda, Zik.

To overcome all enemies:

> Aikn Prmc Dhtr MMPM!

To slay worshippers of the Ancient Ones:

> MASSHANGERGAL

To bind an enemy:

> East, West, North, South,
> Trap his limbs and bind his mouth.
> Seal his eyes and choke his breath.
> Keep him bound thus unto death.

To place a Saxon curse upon an enemy:

> I curse ye by a right line,
> A crooked line, a simple
> And a broken.
> By flame, by wind, by a mass,
> By rain, by clay.
> By a flying thing, by a creeping thing,
> By a serpent.
> By an eye, by a hand, by a foot.
> By a crown, by a cross, by a sword
> And by a scourge.
> I curse thee!

PERCEPTION SPELLS

To know the future:

> Doreh
>
> Orire
>
> Rinir
>
> Eriro
>
> Herod

To see visions in fire:

> Nasi Apis Sipa Isan

To sense any magick or enchantment:

> Horah Osoma Rotor
>
> Amoso Haroh!

To know secrets from beyond the veil:

> BANUTUKUKUTUKKU

To foresee an outcome:

> ARRABABAAL

To remember past lives:

> BALDIKHU

To sense deceit:

> ZIDUR

To sense planar rifts:

> Aramanngi Aranunna!

WEATHER SPELLS

To cause snow to fall:

> Takat, Takat,
>
> Takat, Takat!

To bring rain:

> Sagrir, Sagrir!

To cause thunder:

> Hamag
>
> Abala
>
> Maham
>
> Alaba
>
> Gamah

To summon great storms:

> MASHSHAYEGURRA

To call lightning:

> BAALAGNITARRA

To summon a wind elemental:

> In reatum perjornum yust
> Edorum morani morani est
> Liktus morani. Nervorum
> Femarum este fuenti
> Kilmani majora.

To call multiple lightning strikes:

> Baalagnitarra Gibil!

MISCELLANEOUS SPELLS

To bestow fertility:

Pollicitum pollinis

Pollentia pollinis

Pollentia appollinis

Pollis appollinis

Pollinem polluceo

Polleo polleo

To be chosen:

Helimaz

Feridox

Soladar

To bring sleep:

Morpheus Sopor

Somnificus Somnifer

To be favored by one of rank:

Qebhir

Eraisa

Baqoli

Hiolia

Isliac

Raiaca

To command celestial beings:

Adoshem

Perai

Anexhexeton

Pathumatan

Tetragrammaton

Inessensatoal

Itemon

To cleanse water:

Shabriri!

To overcome befuddlement:

BANUTUKKU

To repel adverse magicks:

MASHSHAMMASHTI

To be revenged:

Raizi

Iziar

Azbgd

Bmmtm

To accelerate crop growth:

AGGHA

To bestow rich harvests:

BURDISHU

To bestow fertility:

Aggabal Gil!

To cleanse ink for magickal use:

> Jod He Vau He Metatron
> Jod Kados Elohim Sabaoth.

To infernally shield your house:

> My home is my fortress,
> And thou art its shield,
> Patrolling its marches,
> Forth thou art sent;
> Who evil would do,
> To thy visage must yield,
> Walk ye my borders···
> Perform my intent!

To reflect magick with a mirror:

> Mirror with power to protect
> I call thee so thou now reflect
> Magick to which I'm now subject.

To enchant a spell sphere:

> Cave, Mountain, Fire, Lake,
> All elements now awake.
> Charge this spell sphere powerfully.
> So it is spoken, let it be.

To bring wealth:

> Fair Lady of the moon
> Bring to me a wealthy boon.
> Fill my hands with coins of gold
> And all the wealth a purse can hold.

To bestow rich harvest:

> Burdishu Hegal!

To break a curse:

> Bubble, bubble··· cauldron bubble,
> Burn this evil, burn this trouble.
> Darkness ends, the curse is done.
> Day has dawned, the fight is won.

To call one to you, if fated to be:

> Av, mi Romani mal,
>
> Pawdel dur chumbas.
>
> Av Kitane mansa?

To be desired:

> Opre the rooker, adre the
>
> Vesh si chiriklo ta
>
> Chirikli; tele the rook
>
> Adre the vesh si piramno
>
> Ta piramni.

BOOK III

SYMBOLS, SIGILS,
&
SCROLLS

Seal Craft

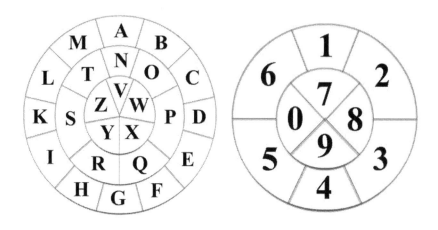

1	2	3	4	5	6	7	8	9
A	B	C	D	E	F	G	H	I
J	K	L	M	N	O	P	Q	R
S	T	U	V	W	X	Y	Z	

To craft a magickal seal, simply draw a
small circle on the first letter of the word.
From the circle, draw a line to the center
of the block for the second letter, then on
to the third. When you reach the final
letter of the word, terminate the line with

another small circle. For multiple words, simply draw the seals directly atop one another so that they intertwine to combine their energies into the desired, combined effect.

If wishing to use the numeric circle, the process is similar, but with an additional, initial step. First, you must convert the command word or words to numbers using any of the accepted forms of numerology. The above table is the most commonly used, and so is a good place to start. Convert the word, letter by letter, to the corresponding numbers. Then, as with the letters, use the numeric circle to map the word and create the sigil.

Runic Correspondence

(Major Arcana)

ᚡ	Tower	ᚷ	Wheel of Fortune
ᚠ	High Priestess	ᛏ	Moon
ᚦ	Emperor	ᛋ	Sun
ᚱ	Death	↑	Justice
ᚲ	Chariot	ᛗ	Magician
✕	Lovers	ᚱ	Star
ᚹ	Strength	☐	Judgement
ᛉ	Devil	ᛕ	Temperance
ᛁ	Hermit	ᛒ	Empress
ᛃ	Hanged Man	ᚺ	World

SPIRIT

WATER   **AIR**

FIRE   **EARTH**

Rune	Spirit	Element
ᛗ	♃	Fire
ᚷ	♓	Water
ᚨ	☿	Water
ᛟ	☽◯☾	Water
ᚢ	♉	Earth
ᛈ	♄	Earth
ᚾ	♑	Earth
ᛜ	●	Spirit
ᛇ	♏	Water
ᛉ	♋	Water
ᚠ	♈	Fire
ᚹ	♌	Fire
□	●	Spirit
ᛃ	☸	Spirit
ᚲ	♀	Earth
ᛏ	♎	Air
ᛒ	♍	Earth
ᛖ	♊	Air
ᛚ	☽	Water
ᚺ	♒	Air
ᚱ	♐	Fire
ᚦ	♂	Fire
ᛞ	○	Air
ᛁ	☽	Water
ᛊ	☉	Fire

Mirgonian Sigils

Dragon

Gryphon

Serpent

Death

Life

Vampire

Mage

Werewolf

Mirgonian Runic Oracle

These runes are to be cast all at once upon a surface. Only the runes that land face up are consulted. If the rune is oriented with the top toward you, the meaning is reversed. Any number of readings may be done to gain a more specific answer to the question asked.

You will attack another. Inverse – you will be attacked

You must defend yourself. Inverse – you will need to defend another.

The beginning of the cycle. Inverse – the end of the cycle.

Peace between friends. Inverse – conflict between friends.

A coming–together of people. Inverse – people being driven apart

Y

You must choose a path. Inverse – you are being forced down a path.

True-faith is involved.

Magick is involved.

Scrolls

When crafting a magickal scroll, there are a few key points to consider. These points are quill type, ink, paper/scroll material, letter formation, and scroll storage. In addition to these, an appropriate trigger must be selected prior to scribing the spell. The language used should be the same as the actual spell to be cast, lest some of the scrolls potency is lost during translation. Remember always, the magus scribing the scroll must maintain the deepest concentration and focus throughout the process.

Quill Types:

Porcupine Quill	Generic protection
Crow Feather	Dark Magick/Attacks
Swan Feather	Healing Spells
Dove Feather	Banishment/Peace
Peacock Feather	Illusions/Beauty
Other	All/lesser potency

Ink Types:

Dragons Blood	Attacks/Harmful
Doves' Blood	Defenses/Beneficial
Human Blood	All/High Potency
Other	All/Lesser Potency

Paper/Scroll Materials:

Paper	Low Potency
Parchment Paper	Medium Potency
Lambskin Parchment	Highest Potency
Leather	Medium Potency
Papyrus	High Potency
Other	Low Potency

When it comes to letter formation, it is extremely important to ensure that every letter is penned neatly and accurately. In the event of an error, the entire scroll must be abandoned and started anew. Text should be neither excessively large nor excessively small. Cramped or poorly written text will render the scroll powerless. It is advisable to practice writing the scroll on scrap paper prior to penning the scroll itself.

Of equal importance to creating the scroll is the manner in which the completed scroll is stored. Improper storage of a spell scroll will result in the scrolls power bleeding away. This would result in the scroll being useless. The energies drawn upon should be taken into consideration when a scroll case is selected.

Scroll Case Materials:

Wood	Nature Magicks
Silver	All/High Effectiveness
Iron	Fairy Magicks
Other Metals	All/Medium Effectiveness
Other Materials	All/Low Effectiveness
Bone	Dark Magicks

Additionally, tying a piece of silk ribbon around the scroll before placing it within a case will greatly reduce the chances of Bleeding. Energy Bleed of a high-potency scroll, can if left unchecked, alter the surrounding area in a way appropriate to the spells' type and energy.

When preparing to create a scroll, consider the circumstances under which it will be used. It is of the utmost importance to select a trigger which coincides with the intended use. Triggers can include, but are not limited to, recitation, tearing, and burning. When a scroll is used, its power is drained. Scrolls can be recharged, however, as long as the scroll is not destroyed during the casting. To recharge a scroll, simply read the spell aloud and cast it upon the scroll and its case. Scrolls written in blood, however, will slowly recharge themselves over time. Scrolls written in blood on hide or leather will recharge far more quickly than any other materials or inks.

Sigils etched or engraved upon a scrolls' case will help to protect and safeguard the scroll. Even scroll cases of lesser materials can be made a great deal more effective through the use of sigils. In fact, these Sigil Cases are greatly sought after by mages for this very reason.

Illumination is the final step in scroll crafting. A scroll's illumination, or illustrations, is used to stimulate the mind along lines conducive to the spell's casting. It can also help to quickly identify the spell written upon the scroll by illuminating it with representative symbology. For example, sharp lines of dark contrast could suggest harmful magicks, but would be inappropriate for a healing scroll. These illustrations can also be used to frame the spell to aid the mages in focusing upon it.

The Scroll-crafting Process:

1.) Select the spell with which the scroll shall be imbued.

2.) Determine and acquire all needed materials.

3.) Practice writing out the spell several times to ensure accuracy.

4.) Practice reciting the spell to ensure proper pronunciation.

5.) Meditate upon the spell and the process of creating the scroll.

6.) Scribe the spell upon the scroll, reciting each word as you complete it before moving on to the next.

7.) Illuminate the scroll with appropriate patterns.

8.) Cast the spell upon the completed scroll. Place the scroll in its selected case.

The completed scroll should remain secure in its case until it is needed. The only time a scroll should be removed is to ensure no bleeding has occurred. If it has, recast the spell upon the scroll and then place it in a more secure scroll case.

Made in United States
Orlando, FL
18 November 2023

39128529R00074